MW01093397

Greater Than a Tourist Book Series
Reviews from Readers

I think the series is wonderful and beneficial for tourists to get information before visiting the city.

-Seckin Zumbul, Izmir Turkey

I am a world traveler who has read many trip guides but this one really made a difference for me. I would call it a heartfelt creation of a local guide expert instead of just a guide.

-Susy, Isla Holbox, Mexico

New to the area like me, this is a must have!

 -Joe, Bloomington, USA

This is a good series that gets down to it when looking for things to do at your destination without having to read a novel for just a few ideas.

-Rachel, Monterey, USA

Good information to have to plan my trip to this destination.

-Pennie Farrell, Mexico

Great ideas for a port day.

-Mary Martin USA

Aptly titled, you won't just be a tourist after reading this book. You'll be greater than a tourist!

-Alan Warner, Grand Rapids, USA

Even though I only have three days to spend in San Miguel in an upcoming visit, I will use the author's suggestions to guide some of my time there. An easy read - with chapters named to guide me in directions I want to go.

-Robert Catapano, USA

Great insights from a local perspective! Useful information and a very good value!

-Sarah, USA

This series provides an in-depth experience through the eyes of a local. Reading these series will help you to travel the city in with confidence and it'll make your journey a unique one.

-Andrew Teoh, Ipoh, Malaysia

GREATER THAN A TOURIST- ZURICH SWITZERLAND

50 Travel Tips from a Local

Isabelle Howells

Cover designed by: Ivana Stamenkovic
Cover Image: https://pixabay.com/photos/zurich-city-marina-2356362/

Image 1: https://commons.wikimedia.org/wiki/File:Limmat.jpg MadGeographer [CC BY-SA (https://creativecommons.org/licenses/by-sa/3.0)]
Image 2: https://commons.wikimedia.org/wiki/File:Z%C3%BCrichsee_-_Enge_-_Uetliberg_IMG_2193.JPG Roland zh, upload on 17. April 2009 [CC BY-SA (https://creativecommons.org/licenses/by-sa/3.0)]
Image 3: https://commons.wikimedia.org/wiki/File:Z%C3%BCrich_-_Augustinergasse_IMG_2046.JPG Roland zh [CC BY-SA (https://creativecommons.org/licenses/by-sa/3.0)]
Image 4: https://commons.wikimedia.org/wiki/File:Bahnhofstrasse_Grieder.jpg sidonius 20:44, 7 June 2006 (UTC) [Public domain]

CZYK Publishing Since 2011.
Greater Than a Tourist

Lock Haven, PA
All rights reserved.

ISBN: 9798613453368

>TOURIST

50 TRAVEL TIPS FROM A LOCAL

BOOK DESCRIPTION

With travel tips and culture in our guidebooks written by a local, it is never too late to visit Zurich. Most travel books tell you how to travel like a tourist. Although there is nothing wrong with that, as part of the 'Greater Than a Tourist' series, this book will give you candid travel tips from someone who has lived at your next travel destination. This guide book will not tell you exact addresses or store hours but instead gives you knowledge that you may not find in other smaller print travel books. Experience cultural, culinary delights, and attractions with the guidance of a Local. Slow down and get to know the people with this invaluable guide. By the time you finish this book, you will be eager and prepared to discover new activities at your next travel destination.

Inside this travel guide book you will find:

Visitor information from a Local
Tour ideas and inspiration
Save time with valuable guidebook information

Greater Than a Tourist- A Travel Guidebook with 50 Travel Tips from a Local. Slow down, stay in one place, and get to know the people and culture. By the time you finish this book, you will be eager and prepared to travel to your next destination.

OUR STORY

Traveling is a passion of the Greater than a Tourist book series creator. Lisa studied abroad in college, and for their honeymoon Lisa and her husband toured Europe. During her travels to Malta, an older man tried to give her some advice based on his own experience living on the island since he was a young boy. She was not sure if she should talk to the stranger but was interested in his advice. When traveling to some places she was wary to talk to locals because she was afraid that they weren't being genuine. Through her travels, Lisa learned how much locals had to share with tourists. Lisa created the Greater Than a Tourist book series to help connect people with locals. A topic that locals are very passionate about sharing.

TABLE OF CONTENTS

FUN FOR ALL THE FAMILY

DEDICATION

This book is dedicated to all my travel partners, past, present and future, who help me explore the world and myself.

ABOUT THE AUTHOR

Isabelle Howells is a Brit, who now lives in Zurich, Switzerland. She emigrated more than ten years ago, when her job brought her to the Land of Milk and Money. During this time, she has become obsessed with exploring the beautiful country that she now calls home.

She loves to travel all over the world, especially if it means discovering new cultures and new foods. When she is not travelling, she enjoys cooking, reading and drinking good wine.

Isabelle is always happy to share travel tips with her fellow explorers so that they can have rich and unforgettable travel memories.

HOW TO USE THIS BOOK

The *Greater Than a Tourist* book series was written by someone who has lived in an area for over three months. The goal of this book is to help travelers either dream or experience different locations by providing opinions from a local. The author has made suggestions based on their own experiences. Please check before traveling to the area in case the suggested places are unavailable.

Travel Advisories: As a first step in planning any trip abroad, check the Travel Advisories for your intended destination.
https://travel.state.gov/content/travel/en/traveladvisories/traveladvisories.html

FROM THE PUBLISHER

Traveling can be one of the most important parts of a person's life. The anticipation and memories that you have are some of the best. As a publisher of the Greater Than a Tourist, as well as the popular *50 Things to Know* book series, we strive to help you learn about new places, spark your imagination, and inspire you. Wherever you are and whatever you do I wish you safe, fun, and inspiring travel.

Lisa Rusczyk Ed. D.
CZYK Publishing

WELCOME TO
> TOURIST

The Limmat in Zürich

Felsenegg from Lake Zürich

Augustinergasse in the old town

The Bahnhofstrasse seen from Paradeplatz

The more one does and sees and
feels, the more one is able to do,
and the more genuine maybe one's
appreciation of fundamental things
like home, and love, and
understanding companionship.

-   Amelia Earhart

With a population of around 400'000, Zurich is the largest city in Switzerland and lies in the German speaking part of the country. It is a very popular place for expats with more than 30% of current residents living in the city being of foreign nationality.

Due to its size and its world-renowned reputation for being the one of Europe's main financial centres, many mistakenly think that it is the capital but that honour goes to the neighbouring city of Bern.

As well as being home to many international companies, Zurich also has strong ties with sport. It is the home of FIFA, the international governing body of football and hosts one of the Diamond League Athletics meetings annually.

Zürich
Switzerland

Zürich Climate

	High	Low
January	39	31
February	43	32
March	51	37
April	59	42
May	67	50
June	73	56
July	77	59
August	76	59
September	68	53
October	58	46
November	47	38
December	41	33

GreaterThanaTourist.com

Temperatures are in Fahrenheit degrees.
Source: NOAA

THE BASICS

1. MONEY MATTERS

Although Switzerland is based in the heart of central Europe, it does not use the Euro as its currency. So, if you are making a tour of European cities, you will need get your hands on Swiss Francs (CHF). A very limited number of stores will accept payments in Euros, but you will be given change back in CHF.

Money can be exchanged at all airports and large train stations in Switzerland. Check before you exchange if there are any hidden fees or commissions. For example, the bank counters at Zurich Airport charge an additional flat fee of 5 CHF on top of any exchange rate commissions for customers who do not have an account with them.

If you need to pay for something in cash, don't worry if you don't have the correct change. Although wireless card payments are becoming more and more common, Swiss people still rely heavily on cash to pay for goods. It is possible to pay for small items with large bank notes. Everyone always has change, so don't feel embarrassed if you don't have anything smaller. Even isolated restaurants on top of mountains will be able to break a 100 CHF note without batting an eyelid.

The Swiss Franc is also accepted in the small principality of Liechtenstein, a beautiful and often overlooked country. It is an hour and a half car journey from Zurich and is worth a visit if you have time.

2. GETTING AROUND

If you arrive at Zurich Airport, the best way to get into the city centre is by public transport. You can either take a train or a tram which depart at regular intervals throughout the day.

In fact, using public transport during your whole stay is more than advisable. All the things you have heard about the transport system in Switzerland are true: it's reliable, clean and good for the environment.

But there must be at least one drawback: as a tourist, it can be an expensive way to travel.

If you are staying in Switzerland for an extended period of time with the intention of utilizing public transport, it is best to invest in a travel card that gives you unlimited access to all rail, road and waterways throughout Switzerland.

Options include travel with a Half-Tax card, which is valid for one month, that will entitle you to half price travel throughout the whole Swiss network, or a Day Pass for either 3, 4, 8 or 15 days for unlimited travel.

You can find all the details on the SBB website, which contains all the information about travelling through the whole of the country.

If you are in Zurich for a smaller amount of time, you should definitely think about purchasing the Zuricard (see tip 7). Or you can buy a ticket from the ticket booths at railway stations or from any of the automatic machines available at all large train stations. All machines are available in German, French, Italian and English so make sure you choose the relevant option by touching the screen at the bottom of the screen before making your choice.

Beware: travelling without a valid ticket is a very expensive business and would be best avoided. If your ticket is not valid you face a minimum fine of 100 CHF plus the cost of a valid ticket for the journey that you are making. Ticket inspectors will also take your details to keep on file and repeat offenders will be fined more heavily.

If you are buying from the ticket machines and are unsure about which ticket you should buy, seek assistance. It will save you a hefty fine!

When you are using public transport, don't worry about missing your stop. On trains, buses and trams there are screens throughout the carriages indicating what the next stop is and regular announcements. Trains from the airport into the city centre also make the announcements in English.

3. APPS TO DOWNLOAD BEFORE YOU ARRIVE

If you are going to be taking advantage of the excellent public transport system, I highly recommend downloading the SBB app. The app is very easy to use and gives you up to date information about the latest arrivals and departures for all modes of transport. Connections as well as the platform information is also clearly displayed.

The best app for weather is MeteoSwiss. The app tends to give more accurate information about the hourly weather than other apps that might already be installed on your phone.

If you want to keep a grip on your finances, make sure that you download the XE currency app. You can select your home currency and up to 10 other currency to convert prices quickly and easily, so this is handy for anywhere you travel.

However, I would advise caution at looking up the prices of everything that you intend to buy. Prices are in Switzerland are known for being more expensive than most of the rest of the world and, if you look up the equivalent price in your home currency, you might be both a little shocked and reluctant to flash the cash. You might only visit Switzerland once in your lifetime so make the most of it. You can always earn more money, but memories can only be made once!

If you don't have data roaming as part of your mobile package, there are lots of places where you should be able to connect to Wi-Fi so that you can use your downloaded apps.

4. STAY SAFE

Switzerland has a very low crime rate and is an extremely safe place to travel by yourself. It's also perfectly safe to walk around by yourself at night.

However, everywhere that attracts tourists, also attracts people who are looking to take advantage of others. I have heard of bags being taken in very busy tourist spots, such as popular restaurants, without the owner even realizing until she came to pay for her meal. So please be as vigilant as you would be anywhere else in the world. The quaint streets and cities can easily lull you into a false sense of security, but you should still be alert to the potential dangers of theft.

Additionally, if you are intending to go hiking and enjoy more of the stunning scenery from a different viewpoint, make sure that you are properly equipped. Check the weather before you set off so that you can take the right clothes with you and make sure that you have enough water and refreshments for the whole trip. Weather in the mountains can change very quickly from one minute to the next so make sure you are prepared for every eventuality.

5. WHO TO ASK FOR HELP

In the unluckily event that you need to contact the emergency services during your stay, here are the numbers of the emergency services:

Police	117
Ambulance	144
Fire	118

If you can't remember the numbers, call 121. This is the central emergency number for Europe. You can call this number anywhere in Europe and they will redirect you to the nearest emergency service.

There are several pharmacies throughout the city in case you need medication that doesn't require a prescription. The pharmacy by the main train station (Zurich Hauptbahnhof) is open every day from 7am until 12 midnight.

If you do need to see a doctor, there is a walk-in clinic next to the pharmacy at the main train station which is designed for travellers or people who are not registered with a family doctor. They can treat most common aliments on the spot and give further advice if needed. The members of the staff can also speak English.

6. USEFUL WORDS AND PHRASES

Zurich is located in the German-speaking part of Switzerland. Although German is one of the four official languages in the country, you will hear the locals speak to each other in a dialect form of German. The dialect differs from canton to canton, so much so that the Swiss sometimes find it difficult to understand their fellow countrymen, despite living a few kilometres away.

However, the most common words and phrases remain the same throughout the German-speaking cantons.

Here are a handful of Swiss German greetings that you might find useful.

Grüzei – Good morning (formal)
Hoi – Good morning (informal)
En Guete! – Bon Appetit !
Prost! – Cheers !
Merci – Thank you
Adieu . Goodbye

Exgüsi – Excuse me

In addition, here are some German words that might be useful for you on your trip in terms of getting around:

Bahnhof – train station

Hauptbahnhof – main train station, abbreviated to HB on maps etc

Apotheke – pharmacy

Strasse – street

Geldautomat – ATM, cash machine

Haltestelle – stop, of a bus, train or tram

Gleis – platform, at train stations

Abfall - waste

7. ZURICH CARD

The easiest, and most cost efficient, way of exploring the city is by buying a Zurich Card. It is a city travel pass which includes the unlimited use of trains, trams, buses boats and cableways in Zurich city and a trip on Lake Zurich on one of the short boat trips. The boat trips give you a unique view of the city and surrounding area and are not to be missed. They leave from Bürkliplatz and run throughout the day.

Holders of the card are also entitled to discounts or exclusive offers at 43 of the city's museums as well as many restaurants and cafes around the city.

Discounts and offers are listed on the website (www.zuerich.com/en/visit/your-city-travel-pass) as well as in the Zurich Card brochure which you can pick up from the main train station or the airport. As offers do sometimes expire or change, make sure that you mention you have the Zurich Card before ordering your meal or drinks.

You can buy these from any ticket machine or from counters at large train stations. If you are arriving at Zurich Airport, the Zurich Card is valid for travel into the city meaning that you can save your money rather than shelling out for an expensive taxi.

The cards can be bought for 24 hours (Adult: 27 CHF / Child: 19 CHF) or 72 hours (Adult: 53 CHF / Child: 37 CHF) depending on how long your stay is.

8. SUPERMARKET SHOPPING

Because Switzerland is expensive, you might want to save some money by visiting a supermarket to buy breakfast or lunch. There are lots of benches and outdoor places to sit during the warmer months where you can enjoy your food. Or, if you are on a self-catering holiday, you will need to visit the local supermarkets.

Coop and Migros are the big players in Switzerland, even though there are lots of other foreigner competitors now entering the market. It is important to be aware of the differences between these two supermarket players. Migros is branded as the family-friendly supermarket and as a result it doesn't sell any alcohol or tobacco products. It took me a while to realize why there wasn't any beer on the shelves there!

Apart from that, both supermarket stock a wide range of food and, in larger stores, other goods, such as clothing and homeware. Both stock an extensive range of chocolates that are great presents for taking home as souvenirs or devouring yourself during the trip.

On a side note, the Swiss do not like to queue at shop tills. So, make sure that you don't get pushed aside or you will find yourself becoming frustrated. This is also valid for queueing at bus stops and railway stations but make sure you let people off the bus or train first before boarding as not doing so is frowned upon.

Many of the supermarket now have self-service checkouts.

9. ENVIRONMENTAL MATTERS

Drinking water is available through the city at the local drinking fountains so there is no need to buy expensive bottled water while you are in Switzerland. Bring your own refillable bottle or instead of throwing your shop-bought water away simply refill it. The water in the fountains has been filtered and is purer than water that you would buy in a supermarket.

There are an incredible 1'200 in Canton Zurich so you will never be too far away from a place to fill up. Also keep a look out for fountains with a small trough at the bottom: these are small fountains to keep dogs well hydrated during the hotter months.

Many of the local supermarkets will charge you for plastic carrier bags and larger paper carrier bags. To cut down on your waste, make sure that you bring a canvas shopping bag with you or reuse carrier bags.

One of the reasons why Zurich has a reputation for being a clean city is the number of containers there are to recycle waste. At many places around the city and at train stations, you can simply dispose of your waste in the containers provided. There are separate compartments depending on if you want to dispose of paper, plastic bottles (PET), tin cans or unrecyclable waste.

10. CROSSING THE ROAD

The Swiss are a law-abiding people and one such rule applies to crossing the road. Even if there is no traffic, Swiss will wait until the green man appears to give the go ahead to cross the road.

Although this causes bemusement to visitors, there is a good reason to follow this rule during your trip. To cross before the green man gives permission is a fineable offence. If a policeman sees you, committing the offence, you will be punished with a heavy fine.

There are also good safety reasons for waiting for permission to cross. In a busy city like Zurich, where the road systems are unfamiliar to you, it is best to wait. Tram and buses seem to come out of nowhere and having a bit of patience is the only way to ensure that you don't get involved in a nasty accident.

Pedestrians have right of way at crossings (where no light signals are in operation), but cars don't always stop when they should. It's best to exercise caution and wait until the cars have come to a stop before crossing.

11. SUNDAY SHOPPING

Don't expect shops to be open on a Sunday. Generally, all shops close on Saturday and don't reopen until Monday morning. Even during the week, shops close before 8pm and won't open until 9am. Workers' rights are heavily protected in Switzerland.

However, you will find some, if not all shops, open on Sundays at busy train stations.

Bahnhofstrasse in Zurich is well-known for being one of the most expensive high streets in Europe and the world. Head out from the main train station and walk towards the lake and see how many designer brands you can see. The closer you get to the lake, the more expensive your shopping bill will be!

12. SOUVENIRS

Many people opt to buy fridge magnets, key rings, cows carved out of wood and T-shirts with them when they go back home.

There is nothing wrong with choosing these as your lasting mementos of your time in Switzerland, but I would recommend something that is more practical and durable, while still remaining quintessentially Swiss. A Victorinox penknife (or army knife) is about as Swiss as you can get.

The centre of Zurich (Rennweg 58, 8001 Zürich) is home to one of the flagship Victorinox stores and has an impressive range of products.

Staff in the shops are always willing to give you their expert advice and make recommendations if you are not sure about what gift you want to buy. Engraving services are also available if you want to make the item even more personal.

Please remember that on your return journey or trip out of the country any knives or similar items should be check into your hold luggage and not in your carry on.

MUSEUMS AND CULTURE
13. SEE AN OPERA

Opera might not be everyone's cup of tea. It has a reputation for being an activity that is only open to the elites and the rich. However, the Opera House in Zurich, located at Sechseläutenplatz by the side of Lake Zurich is changing this outdated opinion.

Ticket prices to see a production are very reasonable. Of course, you can buy tickets for a few hundred CHF but there are also seats available for as little as 35 CHF. They regularly have Open House days when the tickets can be discounted to half price. You can find information for the season on their website, which is available in English.

The inside of the Opera House is worth the entrance fee. The building itself dates back to 1891 and is extremely ornate and decked in gold and red. Before the opera, you can explore the building and get a unique view of the lake from one of the many balconies along the roof.

Don't worry about a dress code. I went in jeans and didn't feel out of place, although there were some people who had made the effort and dressed to impress.

The Opera House organizes an outdoor event on the Sechseläutenplatz called "Opera For All." A cherished part of the Zurich summer crowds gather on the square to enjoy a free performance.

14. CELEBRATE ALL THINGS FOOTBALL

FIFA, the world governing body for the world's most loved sport – football, is headquartered in Zurich. Opened back in 2016, the FIFA museum is dedicated to all things football.

Whether you are a football fan or not, this is definitely worth a visit.

The museum starts in the entrance hall where you can find the football shirt of every team who has taken part in a World Cup. It's an impressive display and everyone is guaranteed to find their favourite team.

The museum is packed with memorabilia, has fun interactive exhibits, such a commentary booths where you can try your hand at commentated on a classic football match, and ends with a series of tests to discover how good your footballing skills are.

There is information about every World Cup tournament and the host nations, as well as information about the Women's World Cup which has been gaining in popularity in recent years.

The highlight of the museum is being able to see the World Cup trophy in all its glory.

15. LANDESMUSEUM

If you want to learn more about the history of Switzerland, this is definitely the place for you.

Permanent exhibitions at this museum include History of Switzerland, Ideas of Switzerland (many famous inventions have been made in here) and Archaeology of Switzerland.

In addition to the permanent collections, normally two or three special exhibitions run concurrently and have different themes.

The museum is open every day, with the exception of Mondays, from 10am.

Entrance fees for adults is 10 CHF which is a bargain considering how many exhibitions there are to see. Children up to the age of 16 get in free.

If you have bought the Zurich Card (as mentioned in tip 7) you just have to show your card to get free entrance.

The museum is located directly behind the main train station.

16. MUSEUM RIETBERG

One of the most highly recommended museums is Museum Rietberg at Gablerstrasse 15, 8002 Zurich.

The museum is the only art museum in the whole of Switzerland that doesn't focus on European art. Its collection includes pieces from Asia, Oceania, the Americas and Africa.

All of the pieces are clearly labelled and dated but if you want more information there are brochures available in each room giving more details about the individual item.

Since 1952 the museum has been housed in the Wesendonck Villa and is surrounded by beautiful gardens which are worth walking round if the weather permits. The building is of historical significance as it is this villa where Wagner is reported to have stayed.

The museum provides lockers where coats and luggage can be stored free of charge.

17. DISCOVER INCREDIBLE ART

This is a must-see for art lovers. I was blown away with the amount of amazing art that is housed in this impressive building. There is everything from Monet to Picasso to Lichtenstein and many others.

Specials exhibitions run concurrently to the permanent collection and should be included in the price of your ticket. It is easily possible to spend more than a few hours appreciating the masterpieces on display.

Photography is permitted in all of the exhibitions but only for private purposed. Any use of flash, tripods or selfie sticks is prohibited so please bear this in mind.

If you want to store any articles of clothing or baggage during your visit, ask a member of staff and they will be able to direct you to the cloakroom.

As well as a museum shop, there is a café selling a range of food and drinks as refreshments.

The museum is located at Heimplatz 1, 8001 Zurich and is a short walk from the lake or it can be reached by tram and bus.

18. WATCH OUT!

The Swiss are known for being a punctual population so there is no surprise that Zurich is home to one of the best watch museums in the country.

The Beyer Watch and Clock Museum documents more than 3'000 years of timekeeping. It's one of the lead private collections of watches in the world and has many rare and valuable items on display. You can find out about every type of watch imaginable as well as scientific navigation devices.

Visitors can find out more about the displayed time pieces interactively via the iPad provided for by the museum.

Entrance fees are 10 CHF for adults, 7 CHF for seniors and 5 CHF for students. Children under the age of 12 are free. If you have bought the Zurich card (as mentioned in tip 7) entrance to the museum is free. The museum is only open on weekdays from 2pm to 6pm.

19. DISCOVER A HIDDEN TREASURE

The North American Native Museum, or NoNAM for short, is a small yet fascinating museum. The museum started off as a private collection and was later acquired by the City of Zurich. Its permanent and special exhibitions never disappoint.

The exhibitions on Seefeldstrasse 317, 8008 Zurich are unfortunately only in German currently, but it is possible to get a guide in English to help you navigate the exhibits.

Some of the areas are interactive which is great for younger visitors.

Like most museums in Zurich, it is closed on Mondays. It's possible to purchase a family ticket (2x Adults, 2x Children) for 25 CHF.

EATING

20. SATISFY YOUR HUNGER AT ZEUGHAUSKELLER

If you are looking for a hearty meal to satisfy your hunger after a busy day of sightseeing, you should head to Zeughauskeller. Located next to Paradeplatz (where many Swiss banks are headquartered) this restaurant is known and loved by tourists and locals alike. On any given day of the week the place will be packed with couples and friends dining out alongside bankers entertaining clients.

The restaurant has an interesting décor. Zeughauskeller means arsenal in English so old weapons, guns and canons can be seen dotted around the room.

The food is simple, very tasty and comes in huge portions so make sure you are ready to put on a few pounds if you want to visit. One of their specialities is Cordon Bleu which comes with mountains of fries on the side. You can also have your meat served to you on a sword skewer.

Make sure you make a reservation if you want to eat here. It is very popular all the time and advance booking is the only way you will be able to guarantee a table at the time of your choosing.

21. BECOME A MAÎTRE CHOCOLATIER

Technically this isn't a recommendation of somewhere to sit down to eat but it does involve eating what you make at the end of the day.

The Lindt factory in Zurich has a Chocolateria for visitors to learn how to make chocolate and create their own cocoa bean inspired creations to take home and enjoy.

From May 2020 the Home of Lindt Chocolate will be opening, giving visitors even more incredible opportunities to work more with chocolate.

It goes without saying that these experiences sell out quickly, so you need to plan ahead and book any of the workshops and experiences you are interested in before you get on the plane to Switzerland.

If you do find that the workshops are all booked out, as an alternative you can visit the Lindt Shop in Kilchberg. This flagship store stocks all your favourite Lindt products and more.

22. EATING CHEESE FONDUE

If you are visiting Switzerland, enjoying a cheese fondue is a must. You can't tell friends and family back home that you travelled all that way and didn't try one of the most famous things about Switzerland.

As a rule, the Swiss only eat fondue in winter but it is available all year round in most traditional restaurants. Some places will allow you to choose which cheese you would like, while others offer a standard mix of cheeses that they use to make the dish.

One of the best places I've had fondue was at Hotel Adler in the centre of Zurich. Throughout the year it is full of tourists who are eager to try this

Swiss staple. The waiting staff are friendly and accommodating and the food is delicious.

As cheese fondue is a heavy meal, I suggest you wash the food down with grappa to help your digestion.

Of course, if you aren't keen to try fondue (and, I admit, I was very skeptical about it when I first tried it but now I love it), they have other traditional Swiss favourites on their menu for you to choose from, like Rösti and Raclette.

You can find the restaurant on Rosengasse 10, 8001 Zurich. It is within walking distance of the main train station.

23. THE NATIONAL SAUSAGE OF SWITZERLAND

If you are feeling hungry and want to pick up something quick, easy but quintessentially Swiss the best thing to do is get your hands on a cervelat.

Known as the national sausage of Switzerland, more than 160 million cervelats are annually. This is the equivalent of 25 cervelats being consumed by every person each year.

Cervelats are cooked by being slightly smoked and then boiled. The taste of the sausages depends on the region, as there are variations in recipes from region to region. Generally, they have a similar taste to that of a frankfurter. Usually they are served with a dollop of mustard and a chunk of bread called a Bürli.

You can sample a cervelat in any of the traditional restaurant in Zurich or at food stalls at the main train station, for example.

24. TASTE THE BEST HOT CHOCOLATE IN TOWN

You can find the best hot chocolate in town and have a delicious cake at the same time by visiting Café Schober on Napfgasse 4.

The café itself was first opened back in 1842 and since then it has gained a reputation for its hot chocolate but also its fantastic range of handmade cakes and sweet delights. This is one place for chocolate lovers to make sure they visit.

There is a small terrace outside which is great in the summer but is also in use during the winter months. I once sat outside with a blanket wrapped around me as the snow fell!

Inside the building is ornately decorated and has several floors each with their own distinctive style and character.

They also have a great lunch and brunch menu if you are looking for something more substantial to eat.

DRINKING

25. HANG OUT WITH THE LOCALS

During the summer plenty of people flock to Frau Gerold's after work to enjoy as much of the summer sun.

The place itself has a very rustic feel to it. Tables and chairs are of a wooden bench-style and the rest is made up of old cargo containers. As well as bars there are street food style stalls selling nachos to vegan burgers.

It is completely open-air, so you do need to have a dry day if you want to enjoy it to the full.

However, the venue is also open during the winter months and has fire pits to keep guests warm and the obligatory hot glass of Glühwein.

It's a stone's throw away from Hardbrücke train station and is easily accessible via public transport.

A handy tip is to go there before 4pm so you can get a seat!

26. UP IN THE CLOUDS

Prime Tower, next to Hardbrücke train station, was officially the tallest skyscraper in Switzerland from 2011 to 2015 until the Roche Tower was completed in Basel. It has a height of 126 metres and is the home well-known companies.

At the very top floor of the Prime Tower is a bar and restaurant called CLOUDS. As well as being an excellent place to unwind with something to eat or drink, it offers a unique viewpoint to see the whole of the city. In fact, the dining area slowly rotates so that dinner guest can enjoy a 360-degree view.

In addition to a restaurant, CLOUDS boasts a chic bistro, bar and smokers lounge. So, there is something for everyone! But you will need to reserve if you want to have a dining experience here.

Currently they offer a Quicklunch from Monday to Friday at the CLOUDS Bistro. They serve a high-quality meal within 25 minutes. No reservation is required for this.

The kitchen also serves a rich brunch buffet on Saturdays and Sundays for 65 CHF.

27. SEE THE HOME OF DADAISM

Cabaret Voltaire in Niederdorf is the home of Dadaism, a philosophical and artistic movement from the early 20th century that was created by European artists who felt that World War I was senseless.

Today the building where this philosophy began still carries on the tradition with live art exhibitions throughout the year.Upstairs there is a well-stocked bar with a great cocktail menu and it is one of the cheapest places in the city for beer.

You can read more about Dadaism here:
https://www.thoughtco.com/what-is-dada-182380

28. OLD CROW

The Old Crow is a bar that is so secret that a lot of the locals don't know it exists. It's a small, intimate bar nestled away in the back streets off Bahnhofstrasse.

It opened in 2013 in Zurich and has since then established itself as one of the best bars in the city. It has a huge range of rare spirits, specializing but not limited to whiskies, and an extensive cocktail list which has something for everyone. Their menus are available online at www.oldcrow.ch

They stand by their motto of "we don't try to offer anything to each guest but a wide selection to a few".

You can find the bar hidden on Schwanengasse 4, 8001 Zürich.

The bar is closed on Sundays and Public Holidays.

29. TALES BAR

If you are looking for a cozy, intimate bar that serves amazing cocktails in a friendly atmosphere then this is the place for you. Opened in 2015, Tales Bar has fast won a reputation of being one of the best run cocktail bars in the city. The owners say it themselves when they invite you to come and be surprised by what they have to offer.

They open from 6pm until 3am during the week, 8pm until 3am on Saturday and our closed on Sundays.

The bar is located on Selnaustrasse 29, 8001 Zürich.

LANDMARKS
30. CLIMB UETLIBERG

Uetliberg is Zurich's mountain, although mountain doesn't seem like the correct word to describe it when it stands at only 880m high. But getting to the top, especially on a clear day, does give you an excellent view of Zurich: from the airport to the lake and beyond.

There are lots of pathways up to the top if you are feeling energetic. The best way to get there is to take a Tram 13 to Albisgütli. At the last stop head up the hill for about five minutes. When you get there, there is a map showing you the various routes to get to the top.

If you are feeling so energetic or have mobility problems, you can take the S10 train from HB to Uetliberg. At the train stop, there is a restaurant, or you can make the ten minute walk further up the hill to the top of the mountain.

At the top of the mountain is a restaurant called Uto Klum. It has a poor reputation with locals as being overpriced so be prepared to pay a bit more or bring refreshments to bring with you.

There are toilets at the top, but you will need to pay 2CHF to use them. There is also a tower that you can climb to enjoy an even more spectacular view over the city but that will also cost 2 CHF.

From the top there are several footpaths you can take if you want to explore further.

31. GET TO THE TOP OF GROSSMÜNSTER TOWER

The Grossmünster Tower is connected to one of the most famous churches in Switzerland. The building dates back to the 14th century. The church is a magnificent building and my favourite part is being able to go up the tower and look out over the whole of the city.

It takes about 30 minutes to get from the bottom of the tower to the top and back down again.

Check on their website to see which days and times the tower is open to climb: https://www.grossmuenster.ch/en/climbing-tower/

It costs 3 CHF for an adult to climb the tower and, for the spectacular views of the lake, river and even Uetliberg, that is a bargain.

If you are a group of more than 5 you can reserve a timeslot online for climbing the tower. But the reservation is binding so make sure you get there on time.

The church is located next to the river at Grossmünsterplatz,
8001 Zürich.

It is also worth visiting the crypt which is free to enter and often houses exhibitions of local artists.

32. BE AMAZED BY ST PETER'S CLOCK

I am still constantly amazed by the clock face of St Peter's Clock. It is such a simple thing but it's something you won't forget. And, unlike most things in Switzerland, it is completely free to enjoy it!

The Church itself is the oldest parish church in Zurich and the foundation walls date back to the 9th century. But that isn't the most amazing thing about the church...

St Peter's Church in Zurich has the largest clock face in Europe measuring 8.7 meters in diameter. When you stand to watch the clock hands turn, you will be amazed at how far the hands move.

You can find the church at St.-Peter-Hofstatt, 8001 Zürich

33. GREEN VANTAGE POINT OVER ZURICH

Nestled in the back streets of the Old Town of Zurich is a square called Lindenhof. The square has a huge historic significance because not only was it the site of a 4th century Roman fort but it was also where the oath sealing the Helvetic Constitution was held in 1798.

Today it is a tranquil location where many people come to enjoy a bird's eye view over the city. As well as giving a great view of the river, lake and Swiss Alps in the distance, it has a fantastic view of one of the most famous technical universities in the world – ETH. This is where some of the world's greatest minds such as Einstein studied.

As it is a public open space, it is open every day, all year round no matter what the weather is like. You can take in the view from Lindenhof, 8001 Zürich before exploring the charming Old Town on your way back to the city centre.

34. SEE THE TIM BURTON HOUSE

The Tim Burton House has recently become a tourist attraction, even though it has nothing to do with the award-winning director.

However, the house looks like it could be set of his latest production.

Just search Google and you will find the address of this spooky house so you can see it in the flesh.

35. TAKE IN THE CHARM OF THE OLD TOWN

The Old Town of Zurich is heaped in tradition and with its cobbled streets and narrow back streets, it is full of the charm and romance you might expect a Swiss city to have.

You won't be short of places to enjoy Swiss cuisine, do some shopping or have a drink as you meander down the streets without having to worry about traffic.

There are so many quirky shops and places to experience that it really is a place you must explore for yourself.

It is only a short walk from the main train station but is a place that you could easily while away a few hours.

SUMMER ACTIVITIES
36. TAKE A DIP IN THE LAKE

The summers in Zurich can be very hot. The best way to cool down is to head for the lake with your swimming costume and a picnic. As soon as the water is above 13C (55F) people will brave the water.

There are specific places along the lake which have facilities such as lockers, showers and refreshments stands. An area to swim is marked out and there may even be slides or other such activities to make use of. This is a 'Badi', the German equivalent of bath. There is a small fee to enter. However, it is possible to go to any spot by the lake, leave your belongings on the bank and get into the water.

The advantage of a badi is that the entry into the lake is usually by means of a ladder. It means it is safer to get in and out. If you decide to go in anywhere off the side, you will normally have to step onto rocks which can be sharp and slippery to get in. Either way you will be able to enjoy a relaxing swim in the lake.

If you don't go to a badi (and there is nothing wrong with that) do remember that you are not alone in the lake. The lake can get busy with boats, kayaks and other traffics so make sure you are aware of your surrounding and do swim into the driving line of a boat by mistake.

37. TAKE A HIKE

There are so many hiking trails in Switzerland that you will never be bored of a new place to go.

All hiking routes in Switzerland are marked out by a yellow "Wanderweg" (hiking route) sign and routes are marked according to difficulty.

One of the best sites for finding a suitable hiking route is: https://www.wandern.ch/ The website contains lots of routes for the whole of Switzerland, estimates the time of the route and how to get there via public transport.

Please remember if you are planning on hiking to take enough food and drinks to last you the day. It is also important to wear sturdy footwear and appropriate clothing for the time of year. Weather in mountain areas can change very quickly so please be prepared for any type of weather.

For hikes a bit further afield, you can try the 5 Lake hike at Pizol which is a much-loved route of many locals and tourists alike. It is easily reachable by public transport.

38. ON YOUR BIKE

Rather than walking through the city, why not speed things up and take a bike with you as you explore?

There are a few companies in the city who offer free bikes to anyone who wants one. One such company is called Züri Rollt. All year round you can hire a bike for free from them. They are located just behind the main train station on Museumstrasse and are open daily from 8am to 9.30pm. They have a large range of bikes to choose from including city bikes, e-bikes and children's bikes.

To hire one of the bikes you will need to show a valid ID and leave 20CHF as a deposit. In the spring and summer, it is more than likely that the bikes will go fast as everyone will want to spend the day cycling around, so you need to get there as early as possible to guarantee that you'll get one.

It is only possible to make reservations if you want to hire 5 or more bicycles. There is a 10CHF non-refundable charge for each bicycle. You can make a reservation by emailing reservation@zuerirollt.ch

39. BOATING ON THE LAKE

If you want to do something to get your adrenaline pumping, why not hire a speedboat and take it for a spin on the lake. It's a very popular activity in the summer and a good way to enjoy the lake away from the crowded shoreline.

Along the lakeside near to the Opera House there are a lot of companies who hire out boats. You will need to leave a photo ID with them before you can take out a boat. The staff will then instruct you as to how to drive the boat and safety instructions and off you go!

Boats can normally be hired for an hour and you can drive anywhere on the lake. You are responsible for being promptly back with the boat at the correct time or you might be charged a late fee. Make sure you keep an eye on the time.

It's also possible to hire pedalo with or without a slide so you can ride into the middle of the lake and jump into the lake. It can be a bit tricky to get back onto the pedalo even using the ladder provided but you will soon get used to it.

40. FIND ADVENTURE AT ALPAMARE

Alpamare is Switzerland largest and best water park and is fun for all the family irrespective of age. There are small pools for younger children and those who are not strong swimmers as well as water slides for the more adventurous.

Each of the slides is graded according to difficulty meaning that smaller children are not able to try the more difficult slides.

As well as a water park, there is an on-site restaurant for refreshments throughout the day and top of the range changing facilities.

You can buy day tickets or tickets for four hours if you don't plan to spend the whole day there. It's cheaper to buy the tickets in advance online than when you get there. If you need to take public transport to the park, there are also great offers to combine your entrance ticket with the price of the train fare making the cost of the trip even better value.

WINTER ACTIVITES

41. ENJOY THE CHRISTMAS MARKETS

Zurich is fast becoming THE destination in Europe because of the incredible Christmas market stalls in the city.

The markets usually start at the end of November and carry on until the first week in January. It seems like the whole city turns into one big Christmassy event because of the amount of Christmas stalls that pop up in this time.

The two biggest Christmas markets can be found at the main train station and is home to a huge Christmas tree that is decorated from top to toe in Swarovski crystals, and by Bellevue at Sechselaütenplatz. Both markets offer a variety of food and drink stalls as well as stalls selling great ideas for gifts. There are also many stalls lining the streets around the main train station.

The markets do get busy during the evenings because many of the locals will descend on them after work for a drink or something to eat.

Landesmuesum, located to the rear of the main station, transforms its outside space into an Illuminarium. All the buildings are lit up and there are plenty of opportunities to buy a hot glühwein and sweet treats.

Make sure you don't miss the singing Christmas tree as well. Local school children sing carols and Christmas songs twice an evening to passersby.

42. HAVE A TASTE AT THE WINE SHIPS

Every year at the end of autumn twelve of the cities' ships are moored at Bürkliplatz for three weeks for a festival of wine. Wine merchants from all around Switzerland come to show their products, which are available to taste before ordering.

The wine on offer is produced in Switzerland as well as the rest of the world. There will be a wine there to stir your palate! As well as the tastings, there are restaurants available to serve Raclette and Fondue at reasonable prices.

The entrance fee is 30 CHF (or 27 CHF if you buy online) and there is no limit to the amount of wine you can taste. It is possible to order the wine on board and have it delivered at a later date and most of the producers are willing to ship orders internationally. Unfortunately, due to restrictions with space, it isn't possible to buy and take away your purchase on the day.

For the latest information and dates, check out their website here: https://www.expovina.ch/

43. TASTE SOMETHING STRONGER AT THE WHISKY SHIPS

Like the wine ships in Tip number 42, the whisky ships are also available to the public at the end of November for whisky tastings. These tasting take place at Bikers Base Eventhalle,
Schanzweg 11, 8330 Pfäffikon.

At the last count there were 27 producers at the event and the number is increasing all the time as Swiss Whisky becomes more and more popular.

How much the event costs depends on how much you want to taste. Entrance fees start at 20 CHF up to 60 CHF and every entrance price includes a souvenir glass for you to take home and keep.

If you are travelling by public transport, there are comprehensive directions available on their website and a free shuttlebus between the train station at Pfäffikon ZH and the event hall is in operation.

For the latest information and dates, check out their website here: https://whiskyschiffzuerich.ch/

44. HIT THE SLOPES

If you are skier or a snowboarder, one of your life ambitions will probably be to ski in Switzerland. Zurich city itself doesn't have any slopes but many famous skiing resorts are a short train ride away.

Flumsberg is an hour away by train. You can rent ski directly at the resort, but it is cheaper to hire them from the city and take them with you on the train. A store like Migros XXX hires out ski and snowboarding equipment for reasonable prices. If you are new to skiing, there is a great ski school at the resort and all instructors speak to a high standard of English.

Going further a field to places like Flims and Davos is also easy by train. Check on the SSB app for details of how to get there by train. SBB sells a 'Snow and Rail' ticket which means you can buy your train ticket in combination with the ski pass for the resort. This will save time queuing up for a ski pass when you get to the resort.

If skiing or snowboarding isn't your thing, you could also give snowshoeing a try. You should be able to rent the snowshoes at the resort.

Many resorts also have sleigh and toboggan runs which are great fun for all the family. There is a way for the whole family to enjoy the snow.

45. ICE STAKING AT DOLDER

The Dolder Grand is the most exclusive hotel in Zurich and every year they have an open-air staking rink for lovers of the ice to enjoy.

The ice is one of the largest ice rinks in Europe and covers 6'000 square meters of ice. At Christmas time there is a huge tree in the centre of the rink which is decorated with thousands of LED lights.

The admission price is 9 CHF for adults and 7 CHF for children. Stakes are available to hire from the rink. Check out the opening times of the rink here: https://www.doldersports.com/en/winter-front-page-en/ice-skating-rink/

There is also the possibility to have lessons and buy souvenirs to remember your trip.

FUN FOR ALL THE FAMILY

46. MONKEYING AROUND AT THE ZOO

Zurich Zoo is a great place for kids and grown-ups alike. Getting to the zoo is very easy. Take a number 6 tram in the direction of the zoo and you only have a short walk to the entrance. The zoo is open 365 days a year.

Highlights at the zoo include the Masoala Rainforest, the newly opened Australasia zone and the Elephant House. In the Elephant House it is possible to see the animals swimming underwater thanks to the reinforced glass alongside the water feature.

On Sundays it is possible to reserve to have brunch in the Elephant House. The restaurant directly overlooks the enclosure and give a great view of the animals while you enjoy a tasty meal.

In winter months there is also a penguin parade, in which the keepers lead the penguins through the zoo so visitors can see them up close.

There is also an app you can download with a map as well as information about when feeding times for the animals and special presentations made by the zookeepers take place. Check on the website for details of when these take place.

47. TAKE A WALK ON THE WILD SIDE

If you want to see native animals in their natural habitat, you should pay Wildnis Park in Zurich a visit. Described as a nature discovery park, it provides undisturbed habitats for animals and plants while allowing visitors to discover nature.

There are different zones where visitors can discover animals such as wild ponies, elks, bears, wolves and wildcats.

The park is totally free to enter but donation to the charity that runs it are appreciated. There is also a Nature Museum onsite which charges a small fee to enter.

Getting to the park is very easy. Take the S4 train, which has an hourly connection throughout the year, or Bus 137, which is operational from March to October.

The park is closed on Mondays but is open the rest of the week from 9am.

48. TRIP TO RAPPERSWIL

If you want to get out of the city and explore a smaller town, I would highly recommend a trip to Rapperswil. It is a small town situated on Lake Zurich and you can either take a train from the main station or take the more scenic route and hop on a boat at Bürkliplatz. However, please be aware the boats are not fully operational during the winter months of November to March.

Even though Rapperswil itself is small, it has a great deal to offer visitors. Highlights include:

- The Rose Gardens that are situated near the marina. It can be viewed in less than an hour and contains over 16'000 roses.

- The Schloss Rapperswil (Rapperwil Castle) a 13th century structure is open for visitors to explore. It is also home to a deer park where visitors can see the deer wandering and going about their business.

- Knie's Children's Zoo where the family learn more about animals. There is also the possibility to have camel rides, elephant rides and have your picture taken with a sealion.

With all this to do and more it is the perfect place for the whole family to be entertained.

49. HOP ON A TRAIN TO LUCERNE

Lucerne is one of my favourite cities in Switzerland and is well worth a visit. It is an hour journey by train from Zurich with trains leaving regularly during the day.

Highlights not to miss are:

• The Lion Monument which Mark Twain said "(is) the most mournful and moving piece of stone in the world."
• Walk along the Chapel Bridge and check out its hidden art
• Visit the Swiss Transport Museum which is one of the most highly recommended museums in the area
• A boat trip on Lake Lucerne – the boats leave from just outside the train station.

As well as the usual town and city attractions, the city is also surrounded by mountains. You can take public transport to the top of the mountains to enjoy the scenery and fresh air or, if you are feeling more adventurous, enjoy a hike on one of the many hiking routes. The most well-known mountains in the area are Rigi and Pilatus. They offer stunning views of the area, especially on clear days.

50. ENJOY THE FRENCH-SPEAKING PART OF SWITZERLAND

Lausanne is in the French-speaking part of Switzerland and lies off the coast of Lake Geneva and is around two and a half hours away by train. Its cobbled streets and town squares are completely charming.

Highlights not to miss are:

• The stunning Cathedral of Notre Dame in the centre of the city
• The Olympic Museum at Quai d'Ouchy 1, Lausanne 1006, which tells the history of the Olympic Games, has huge amounts of memorabilia and explains how modern athletes prepare for the games, is great fun and educational for all the family

Lausanne is also perfectly placed for a further onward trip to Geneva, the biggest city in the French speaking part of the country, or to Vevey where Charlie Chapin lived and is now a museum, or to Montreux, the home of the famous jazz festival and where the band Queen and other stars recorded their most famous records.

BONUS TIPS

Here are some bonus tips for some special events happening each year in Zurich.

Sechsaluten

A tradition in Zurich dating back to medieval times, this festival takes place every third Monday in April. At 6pm a huge bonfire, on which a snowman sits, is lit. The snowman's head is filled with firecrackers and, legend has it, that the quicker it takes for the snowman's head to explode, the warmer the summer will be. After the bonfire dies down, it is customary for the locals to use the embers of the fire to grill sausages for dinner.

Limmatswimm

Every summer one weekend is dedicated to Limmatswimm when participants jump into the River Limmat and swim from the mouth of the river until Letten with floating devices on a nautical theme. It's a great event to witness but even better to take part in. Tickets for the event go on sale a few weeks before the event but they do sell out quickly.

Diamond League Athletics

Taking place towards the end of the outdoor season, Zurich is home to one of the final meets of the athletic season. Tickets for the event do sell out quickly but it is worth a trip for any lover of athletics to get a taste of life track side. Check the Diamond League Athletics calendar to find the next meeting.

TOP REASONS TO BOOK THIS TRIP

Culture: Music, art and museums offerings are unforgettable.

Food: The food is really something special and everyone dreams about eating fondue while in sight of the Swiss Alps, don't they?

Fun for all the Family: There is so much to enjoy no matter how old or young or what time of the year it is.

DID YOU KNOW?

With a population of 400'00, Zurich is the largest city in Switzerland.

Switzerland has four official languages: German, French, Italian and Rhaeto-Romantsch.

Coffee in Zurich is the most expensive in the world, according to the Coffee Price Index in 2016.

Swiss law prohibits owning social pets unless you have two of them. It is illegal to own just one guinea pig, mouse, canary, ferret, fish, pig or another social creature.

Switzerland is home to 208 mountains over a height of 3'000m.

Switzerland is also known as the Confoederatio Helvetica which is why it has the abbreviation CH.

Military service is compulsory for all Swiss citizens. Male citizens are required to serve in the army after the age of 18. Woman can opt to volunteer to do the same amount of service as their male counterparts.

Switzerland's Gotthard tunnel is the longest tunnel in the world. It measures 57km in length.

Switzerland is not governed by one head of state. Instead it has a seven-member executive council that serves as the Swiss collective head of state. From the executive council a president is elected who serves a one-year term.

The Swiss eat more chocolate than any other nation in the world – an average of 11kg per head per year!

PACKING AND PLANNING TIPS

A Week before Leaving

- Arrange for someone to take care of pets and water plants.

- Email and Print important Documents.

- Get Visa and vaccines if needed.

- Check for travel warnings.

- Stop mail and newspaper.

- Notify Credit Card companies where you are going.

- Passports and photo identification is up to date.

- Pay bills.

- Copy important items and download travel Apps.

- Start collecting small bills for tips.

- Have post office hold mail while you are away.

- Check weather for the week.

- Car inspected, oil is changed, and tires have the correct pressure.

- Check airline luggage restrictions.

- Download Apps needed for your trip.

Right Before Leaving

- Contact bank and credit cards to tell them your location.

- Clean out refrigerator.

- Empty garbage cans.

- Lock windows.

- Make sure you have the proper identification with you.

- Bring cash for tips.

- Remember travel documents.

- Lock door behind you.

- Remember wallet.

- Unplug items in house and pack chargers.

- Change your thermostat settings.

- Charge electronics, and prepare camera memory cards.

READ OTHER
GREATER THAN A TOURIST
BOOKS

Greater Than a Tourist- Geneva Switzerland: 50 Travel Tips from a Local by Amalia Kartika

Greater Than a Tourist- St. Croix US Birgin Islands USA: 50 Travel Tips from a Local by Tracy Birdsall

Greater Than a Tourist- San Juan Puerto Rico: 50 Travel Tips from a Local by Melissa Tait

Greater Than a Tourist – Lake George Area New York USA: 50 Travel Tips from a Local by Janine Hirschklau

Greater Than a Tourist – Monterey California United States: 50 Travel Tips from a Local by Katie Begley

Greater Than a Tourist – Chanai Crete Greece: 50 Travel Tips from a Local by Dimitra Papagrigoraki

Greater Than a Tourist – The Garden Route Western Cape Province South Africa: 50 Travel Tips from a Local by Li-Anne McGregor van Aardt

Greater Than a Tourist – Sevilla Andalusia Spain: 50 Travel Tips from a Local by Gabi Gazon

Children's Book: *Charlie the Cavalier Travels the World* by Lisa Rusczyk Ed. D.

> TOURIST

Follow us on Instagram for beautiful travel images:
http://Instagram.com/GreaterThanATourist

Follow *Greater Than a Tourist* on Amazon.
>Tourist Podcast
>T Website
>T Youtube
>T Facebook
>T Goodreads
>T Amazon
>T Mailing List
>T Pinterest
>T Instagram
>T Twitter
>T SoundCloud
>T LinkedIn
>T Map

> TOURIST

At *Greater Than a Tourist,* we love to share travel tips with you. How did we do? What guidance do you have for how we can give you better advice for your next trip? Please send your feedback to GreaterThanaTourist@gmail.com as we continue to improve the series. We appreciate your constructive feedback. Thank you.

METRIC CONVERSIONS

TEMPERATURE

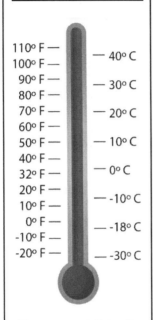

110° F — — 40° C
100° F —
90° F — — 30° C
80° F —
70° F — — 20° C
60° F —
50° F — — 10° C
40° F —
32° F — — 0° C
20° F —
10° F — — -10° C
0° F —
-10° F — — -18° C
-20° F — — -30° C

To convert F to C:

Subtract 32, and then multiply by 5/9 or .5555.

To Convert C to F:

Multiply by 1.8 and then add 32.

32F = 0C

LIQUID VOLUME

To Convert:...............Multiply by
U.S. Gallons to Liters............... 3.8
U.S. Liters to Gallons 26
Imperial Gallons to U.S. Gallons 1.2
Imperial Gallons to Liters....... 4.55
Liters to Imperial Gallons 22
1 Liter = .26 U.S. Gallon
1 U.S. Gallon = 3.8 Liters

DISTANCE

To convert ....Multiply by
Inches to Centimeters 2.54
Centimeters to Inches 39
Feet to Meters...................... .3
Meters to Feet 3.28
Yards to Meters 91
Meters to Yards 1.09
Miles to Kilometers 1.61
Kilometers to Miles............ .62
1 Mile = 1.6 km
1 km = .62 Miles

WEIGHT

1 Ounce = .28 Grams
1 Pound = .4555 Kilograms
1 Gram = .04 Ounce
1 Kilogram = 2.2 Pounds

TRAVEL QUESTIONS

- Do you bring presents home to family or friends after a vacation?

- Do you get motion sick?

- Do you have a favorite billboard?

- Do you know what to do if there is a flat tire?

- Do you like a sun roof open?

- Do you like to eat in the car?

- Do you like to wear sun glasses in the car?

- Do you like toppings on your ice cream?

- Do you use public bathrooms?

- Did you bring a cell phone and does it have power?

- Do you have a form of identification with you?

- Have you ever been pulled over by a cop?

- Have you ever given money to a stranger on a road trip?

- Have you ever taken a road trip with animals?

- Have you ever gone on a vacation alone?

- Have you ever run out of gas?

- If you could move to any place in the world, where would it be?

- If you could travel anywhere in the world, where would you travel?

- If you could travel in any vehicle, which one would it be?

- If you had three things to wish for from a magic genie, what would they be?

- If you have a driver's license, how many times did it take you to pass the test?

- What are you the most afraid of on vacation?

- What do you want to get away from the most when you are on vacation?

- What foods smell bad to you?

- What item do you bring on ever trip with you away from home?

- What makes you sleepy?

- What song would you love to hear on the radio when you're cruising on the highway?

- What travel job would you want the least?

- What will you miss most while you are away from home?

- What is something you always wanted to try?

- What is the best road side attraction that you ever saw?

- What is the farthest distance you ever biked?

- What is the farthest distance you ever walked?

- What is the weirdest thing you needed to buy while on vacation?

- What is your favorite candy?

- What is your favorite color car?

- What is your favorite family vacation?

- What is your favorite food?

- What is your favorite gas station drink or food?

- What is your favorite license plate design?

- What is your favorite restaurant?

- What is your favorite smell?

- What is your favorite song?

- What is your favorite sound that nature makes?

- What is your favorite thing to bring home from a vacation?

- What is your favorite vacation with friends?

- What is your favorite way to relax?

- Where is the farthest place you ever traveled in a car?

- Where is the farthest place you ever went North, South, East and West?

- Where is your favorite place in the world?

- Who is your favorite singer?

- Who taught you how to drive?

- Who will you miss the most while you are away?

- Who if the first person you will contact when you get to your destination?

- Who brought you on your first vacation?

- Who likes to travel the most in your life?

- Would you rather be hot or cold?

- Would you rather drive above, below, or at the speed limited?

- Would you rather drive on a highway or a back road?

- Would you rather go on a train or a boat?

- Would you rather go to the beach or the woods?

TRAVEL BUCKET LIST

1.

2.

3.

4.

5.

6.

7.

8.

9.

10.

NOTES

Made in the USA
Middletown, DE
18 February 2022